Foreword

This book is about a person who has built his own construction company, starting from the work of a simple sewage line worth only 10,000 rupees to doing the work of Crores in and outside India. This story is about a man who once walked kilometres away from his village, but now he owns luxurious cars. There was a time when for feeding his family of 12 members he worked day and night, but today he feeds approximately 20 lakh people per year. In this book we are going to know about a man who never gave up in life, never lost his will power and today he owns one of the greatest construction companies in India. As we move forward in the book we are going to know about all his struggles and few small happy moments of his life that become memories to cherish for the lifetime.

THE INITIAL YEARS.

Born on *VijayaDashmi*, 1954, 7 Oct, Wednesday in a village called '*Rangarh*' which is his mother's home. It was a day of celebration for the family. Father Late Shri Ramanuj Mishra was in the police department posted in Maharashtra, *Wardha*. He completed primary education in Maharashtra but, due to bad health conditions of his mother, father had to resign from police and came back to his home village known as '*Garhwa*', M .P. His Father was very strict and was very conscious about his studies so he enrolled his name to a school which was very good but far from his home, so he had to walk 5 Km everyday to school. He did his middle and high school in a nearby town called *Garh* for which he has to swim and cross a small river and thereafter walk for around

8 km. To do his college he finally moved from a small village to city *Rewa* with all his family consisting of **7 brothers, 3 sisters and parents**, where his Father worked as a 'conductor' in a bus company. Vijay has to manage all his household with his brother and sisters, as his mother was unwell. Coming from not so good background, he has managed to get degree of BSc and MSc in Arts followed by LLB from *Thakur Ranmat Singh collage* (TRS), *Rewa*. Also he was an under officer in NCC, he did the Annual training camp in a place called *Hata*, it was of 15 days under Sikh regiment training camp where he got to learn discipline for life that had made him the person he is today. He passed NCC with 'C' Certificate from NCC. NCC played a vital role in giving him inspiration for doing the social service and

serving the nation through whatever work he does in his life.

While he was in grade 10 on 5th July,1970, he was married to daughter of Late Shri Ugrabhan Ram Pandey, who was a poor farmer from a very small village in M.P named *Pakra*. This was an era when child marriage was followed, so he was married to a 10 year old girl '*Manwati*'. She was the only daughter among 4 sons.

Post completing his graduation, Vijay served as a professor in a private collage of Mauganj (a nearby town having college facilties) only for a period of 6 months with a salary of only 100 rs. But destiny had other plans for him.

But, Vijay thought that he had wasted all his father's hard work who sacrificed all his life just to provide good studies and good life to the best possible way he could.

So, with the guilt of resigning his job only in few months he moved to the capital of the state i.e. Bhopal. He felt ashamed of asking for money from his father so his mother provided him 100 rupees for travelling from Rewa to Bhopal. After arriving in Bhopal he stayed in MLA circuit house in Bhopal because one of MLA was from Rewa and was known to him. After 2 month he finally found the job of a clerk in in PHE department Bhopal .

There he got salary of 150rs per month. To take that salary he walked all the way from circuit house to Kolar for 12 Km. Here also, as fate would have it he quit his job in 6 months. Afterall these experiments, Vijay decided to pursue Law in Rewa as a full time Lawyer.

As life is full of ups and downs, one such incident of his life has completely changed him. While he was working as a lawyer in Rewa, one day one of his relative came to him asking him to make an affidavit, at that time the fee for making one was 60rs but as he was known to him, he took only 20rs. When his senior came to know this he asked him to plead 7 time and also told him to leave the job. He started wondering about the same relative, who was 10th fail and started a business for favouring whom he was fired from his job. He also took inspiration from him and started his own construction business which has become his final destiny. He registered the company in 1979, on his name Vijay Kumar Mishra & Company which later on turned in Vijay Kumar Mishra Construction Pvt Ltd (VKMCPL). As a thousand kilometres journey starts with one single step. It was that one step.

THE FIRST FEW PROJECTS..

He got his first work in *Mauganj* in a project under Ramsagar Dam scheme. It was of Rs 10,000. He didn't asked for money from anyone though he had less money, he somehow managed to execute the job within the time period and got praised for his work from the employer department. His second work was *Belha* dam also in *Mauganj* and subsequently third work of Turra dam in *Sidhi* MP. From there onwards the business began to expand. One man who was always there from the very point of starting his business journey was his brother in law Shri R P Pandey. Later on, with each year passing, his brothers started joining him giving him more strength to expand his business. Among the seven brothers Ashok Mishra, Shailendra Mishra, Ramakant Mishra and the youngest Arvind Mishra joined him in this journey and strengthen him.

During this tenure, VKMCPL has grown his wings in districts like *Shahdol, Anuppur, Amarkantak* and *Beohari* (area in M.P). The company got a dam project named Pondibandha which has given him the financial freedom to play some more risk in expanding the business outside MP. The business expanded day by day without any compromise in the quality of work. However, there were many ups and downs the company had faced till date but had never lowered their Moral of serving the nation with the best way possible.

At that time his family was living near *'Ali Ahmed'* garage in a rental home (area in Rewa). Manwati use to take care of all the family members and consider her brother in laws as her sons. In 1990, Vijay's family finally moved to their own home in Dwarika Nagar in Rewa.

PICTURE GALLERY

Pandit Shree Ramanuj Mishra (Vijay's father, on the left side)

Pandit Shree Badriram Mishra (Vijay's grandfather , on the right side)

Vijay on his Site Visit (Wearing a Skin coloured flat cap)

His three brothers who were involved in business . Mr Ashok , Mr Arvind and Mr Shailendra .

Mr Arvind Mishra there on the working site of Sidhi road.

The Grihapravesh ceremony, done by Manwati when they finally shifted to Dwarika Nagar.

THE 1st TURNING POINT..

1994 he suffered with the **fracture of hip joint** . At that time there was no one to help help . except his parents and wife . His wife just had two sarees which she wore for that whole year. At the same time there was one more such business contractor Mr Umashankar Shukla (he is a relative of current Deputy Chief minister of M.P Mr Rajendra Shukla) . He asked Vijay to do a contract ,eventhough he was fractured he didn't say no . he worked hard in partneship with him but at the end the partnership was broken and Vijay got only 60,000 per year and U.S Shukla treated as if he is just a staff of his company . The struggle for money for his joint surgery was such that his wife spent whole year by just wearing a single saree and eating just one meal in whole day . he borrowed money from his close relatives and promised to return them with interest he got operated in Mumbai and due to his faith in god , his operation was a success. After the operation, as promised he returned all the money with interest.

The wheels of the company again started to move, started to move AGAIN!!!

THE WHEELS START TO MOVE AGAIN..

In 1998 he got a new project in *khargon* which was thousand kilometers away from rewa . He travelled all the night to reach the working site .From the hardwork of company the structure of dam was complete , but wasn't spared by nature. in the month of May due to heavy rain and thunderstorm the structure of dam broke , the company was in great loss. At that time also Vijay didn't lost his will power and made the dam again. That dam benefitted the company so much that after that project the company's turnover finally moved from lakhs to crores.

There was one SDO named Vinod Kumar Khare . he helped the company in every hard times starting from the Shahdol work and when he retired, whole VKMCPL company gave him a farewell party in hotel *Shark inn Resort* in Rewa . In 2004 to 2008 , the company started the projects of World Bank Scheme . The work spread in different locations such as Halali dam, Vidisha over bridge etc. At time Vijay bought a brand new Nissan X Trail which were only two in M.P

From 2006 the eldest son of him Vineet Mishra commonly called as Dadabhai, he is a civil engineer and has taken a degree of BE from *BIT Bhilai* , joined the company Which reduced the work load for him .

V.K Khare's farewell party in Hotel Shark inn (Mr V.K in the centre wearing a cream coloured suit and a pair of spectacles . Vijay on the second number from the right most side)

Vineet on the right hand side . He has been recently launched in the company.

THE 2nd TURNING POINT..

In 2007 , There was an IAS officer named Mr. Radhe Shyam Julania. He was misguided and there were some miscommunication between him and the company. He took some incorrect and misguided actions against the company which caused the company in great loss. He dismissed some of the big projects of the company. Both father and son worked day and night and didn't give up, he and Vineet worked hard again to find some more projects and made them success. But after this mishappening the company suffered great loss .

THIS SIDE OF HOME..

1984 while Vijay was busy in the Pondibandh project his eldest son Vineet was born. he did his schooling In Rewa from ECI school and did his engineering from civil in BIT college In Bhilai. He was married in 2010 to Jyotsna Tripathi daughter of Dr R.S Tripathi and Laxmi Tripathi. In 2012, when Vikas joined the company. The eldest son of Vineet and that generation was born his name was Vansh Vijay Mishra. After 5 years in 2017 Vineet's daughter was born, her name is Vedika Mishra.

In 1986, his daughter was born. Her name was Vibha Mishra she also completed her schooling from ECI school Rewa. She did one year coaching for NEET in Kota, completed her MBBS from D.Y Patil in Pune and did PG from RD Gardi Medical Collage , Ujjain. She is an *Anesthesist* by profession. She is married to Dr Ankit Dadheech son of Dr Narottam Dadheech and Vimla Dadheech. She Is having two children one is Aaryash Dadheech and the other one is Sia Dadheech.

In 1988 Vijay's youngest son was born and his name is Vikas Mishra. He did his schooling from Jyoti School rewa. He is also a civil engineer and has a B.Tech degree from Chennai and has done his M.S degree from Shaffield Hallam University in London. He is married to Dr Monisha Mishra daughter of Suresh Tiwari and Aruna Tiwari in 2017. He has a son whose name is Viren Vijay Mishra.

PICTURE GALLERY

Vijay with his first son Vineet and Manvati .

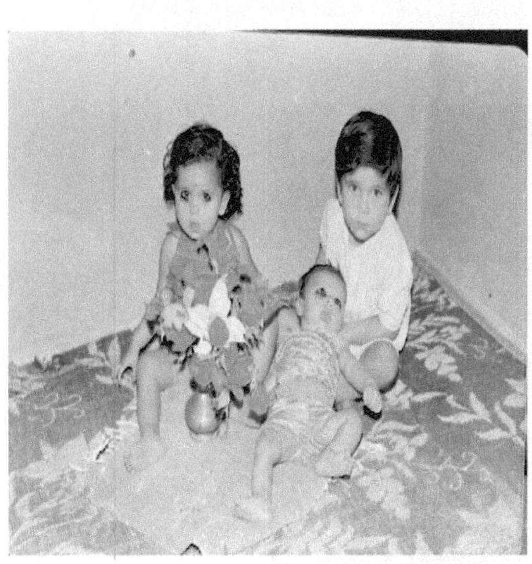

Vineet with Vikas (on his lap) and Vibha (on the left side).

Shree Ramanuj Mishra (Vijay's father) , Shreemati Vedvati Mishra (Vijay's mother) with all the children of the family.

This is the whole family .

"Determination. Hardwork. Vision. Discipline. The Path to Greatness"

-Vijay .K. Mishra.

About the 'AUTHOR'

My name is Vansh Vijay Mishra and I am the grandson of Mr Vijay Mishra . This is my first book which is based on the life of my grandfather . So if there is any printing issue, grammar mistakes or any problem, please give me your feedback .

Regards.

www.ingramcontent.com/pod-product-compliance
Lightning Source LLC
Chambersburg PA
CBHW020657160726
47991CB00003B/1231